Happy Easter to:

Easter Activities for Kids

Connect the Dots Numbers Game
Rebuses
Mazes
Coloring

Mary Lou Brown
Sandy Mahony

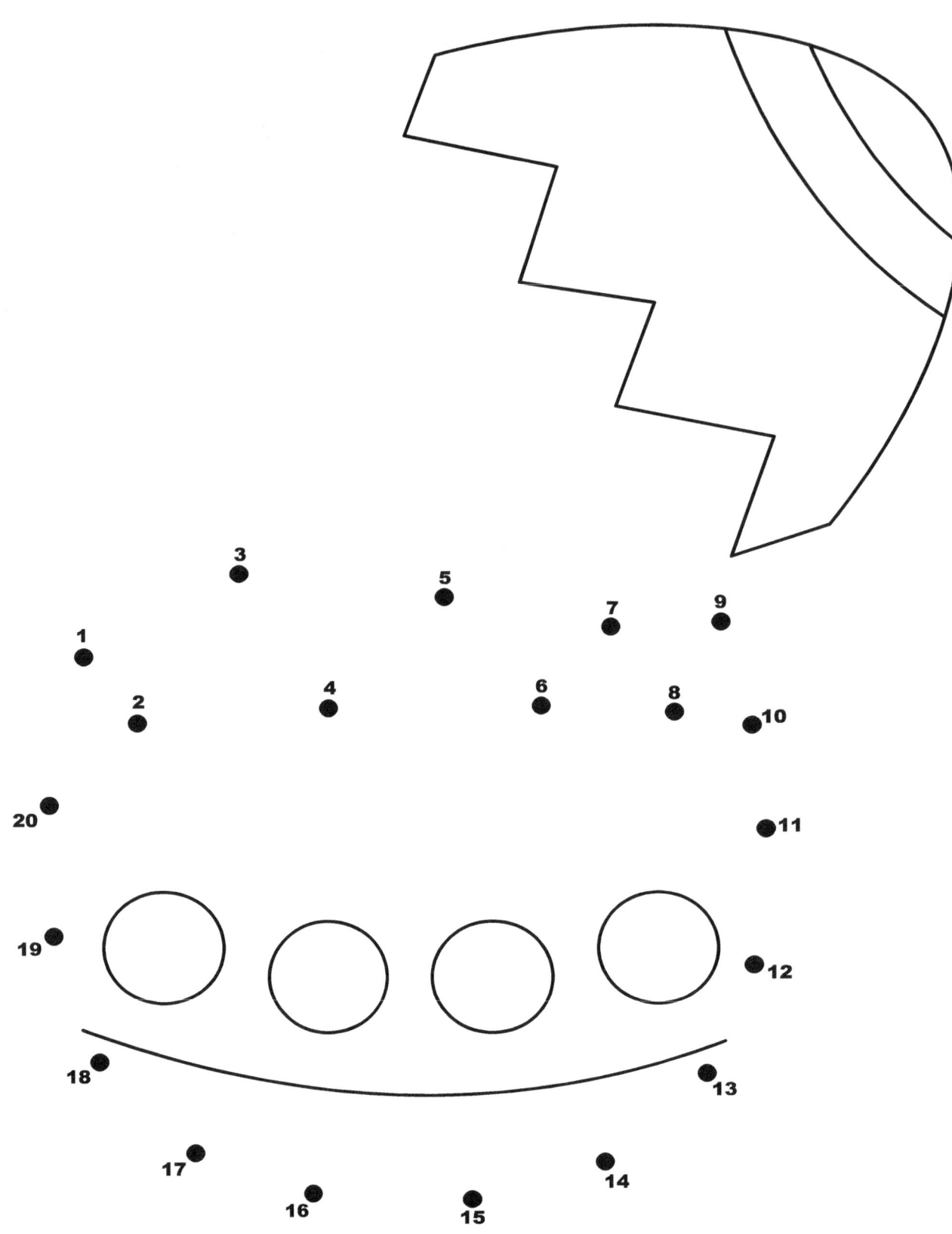

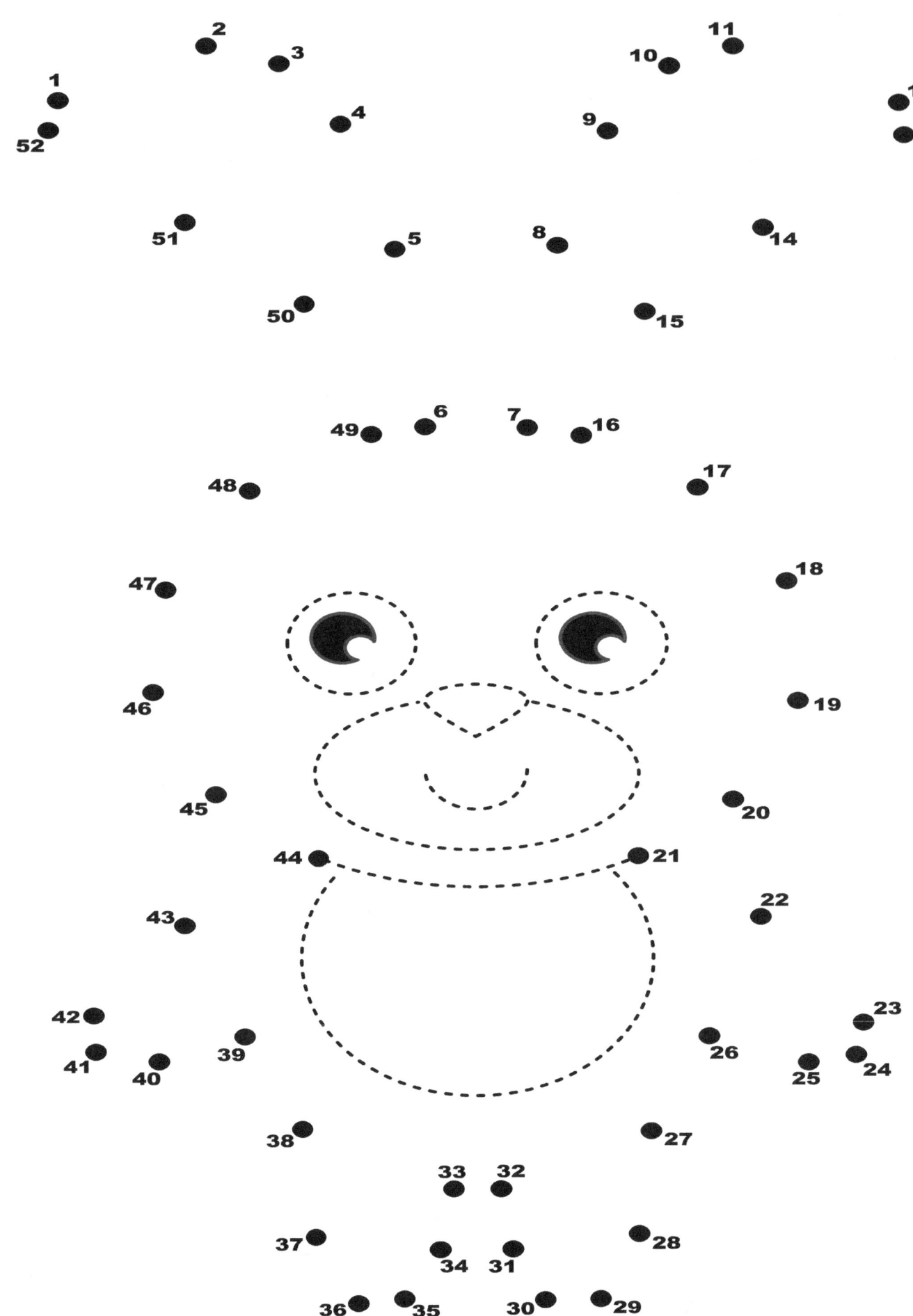

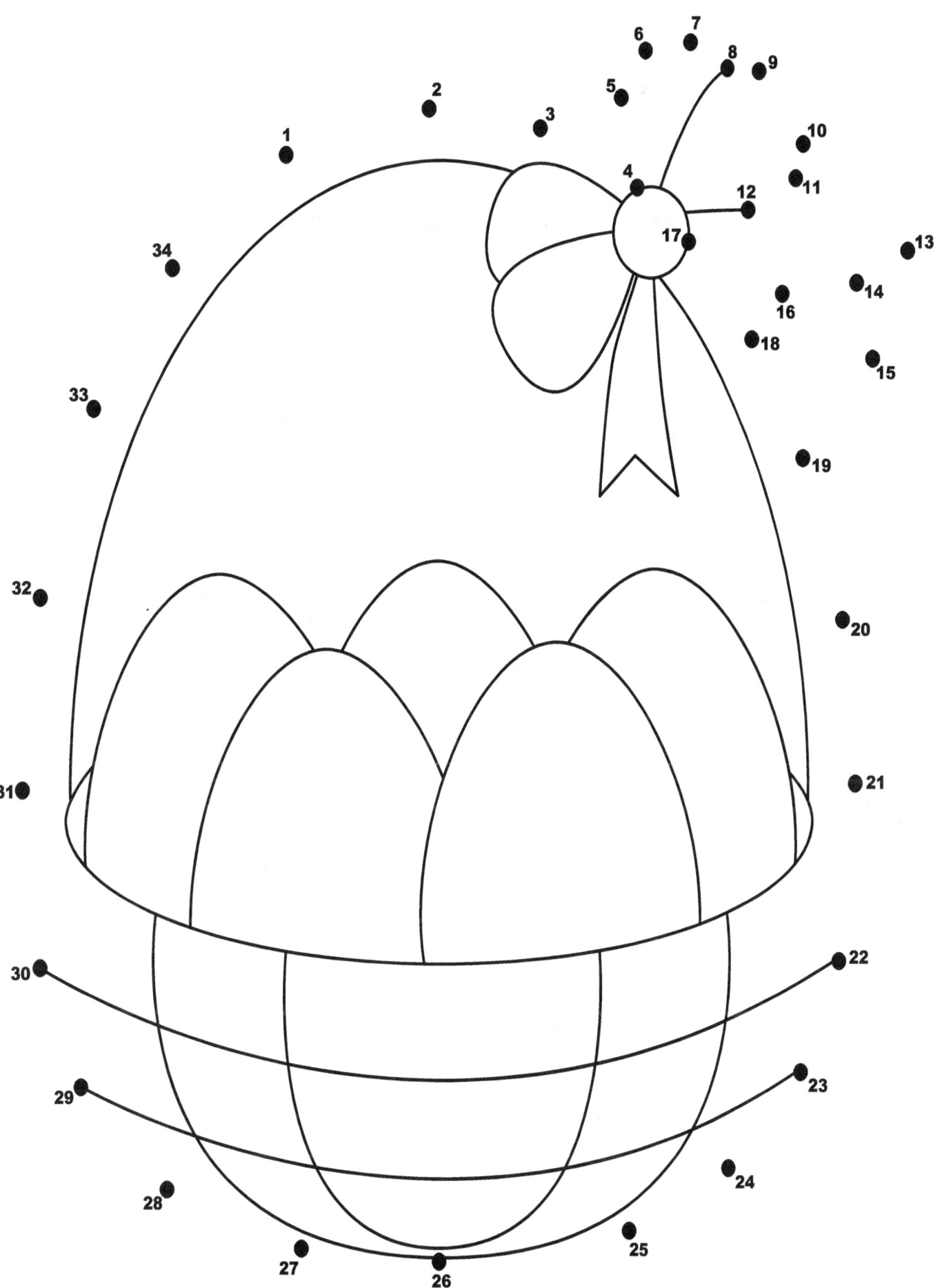

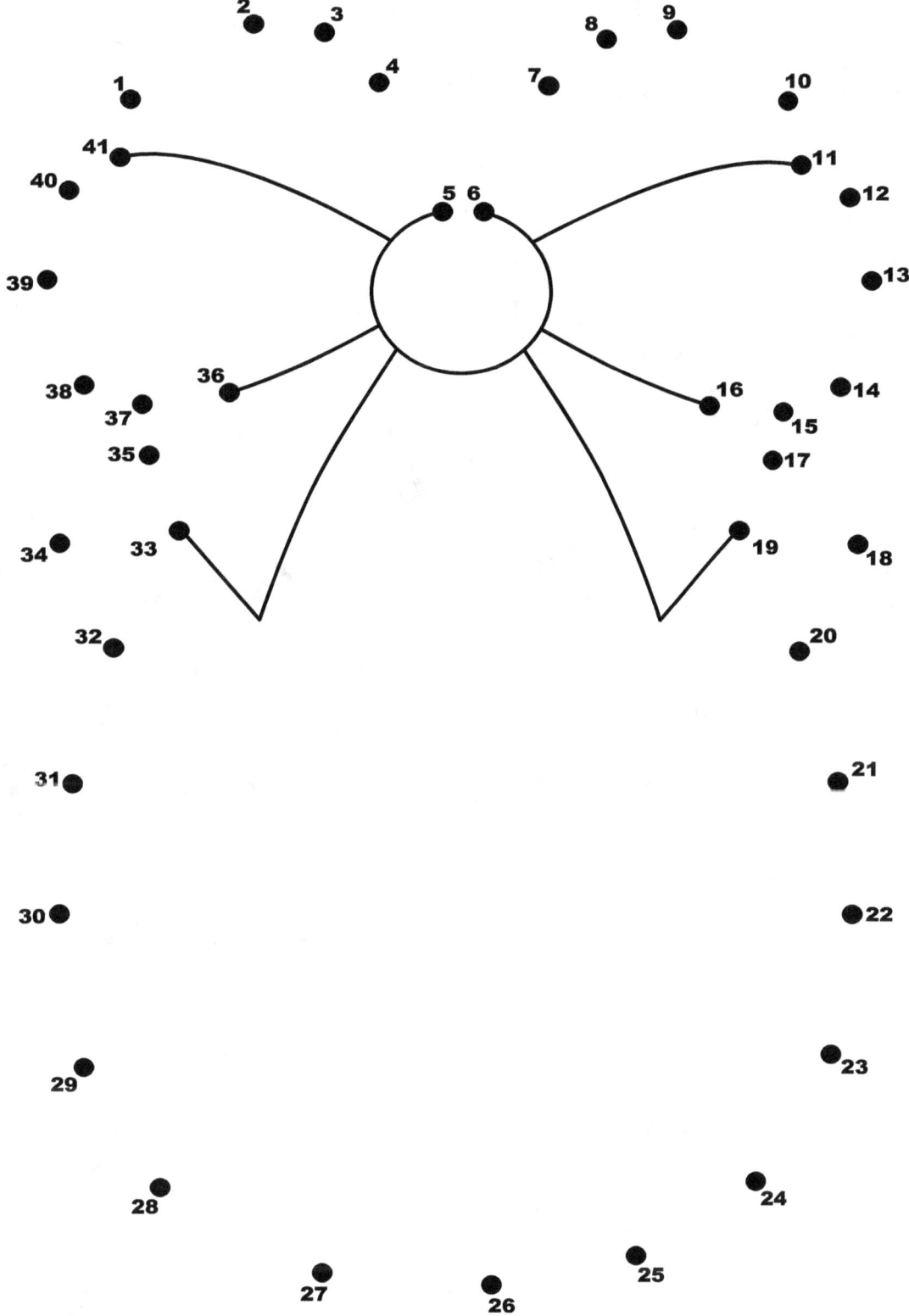

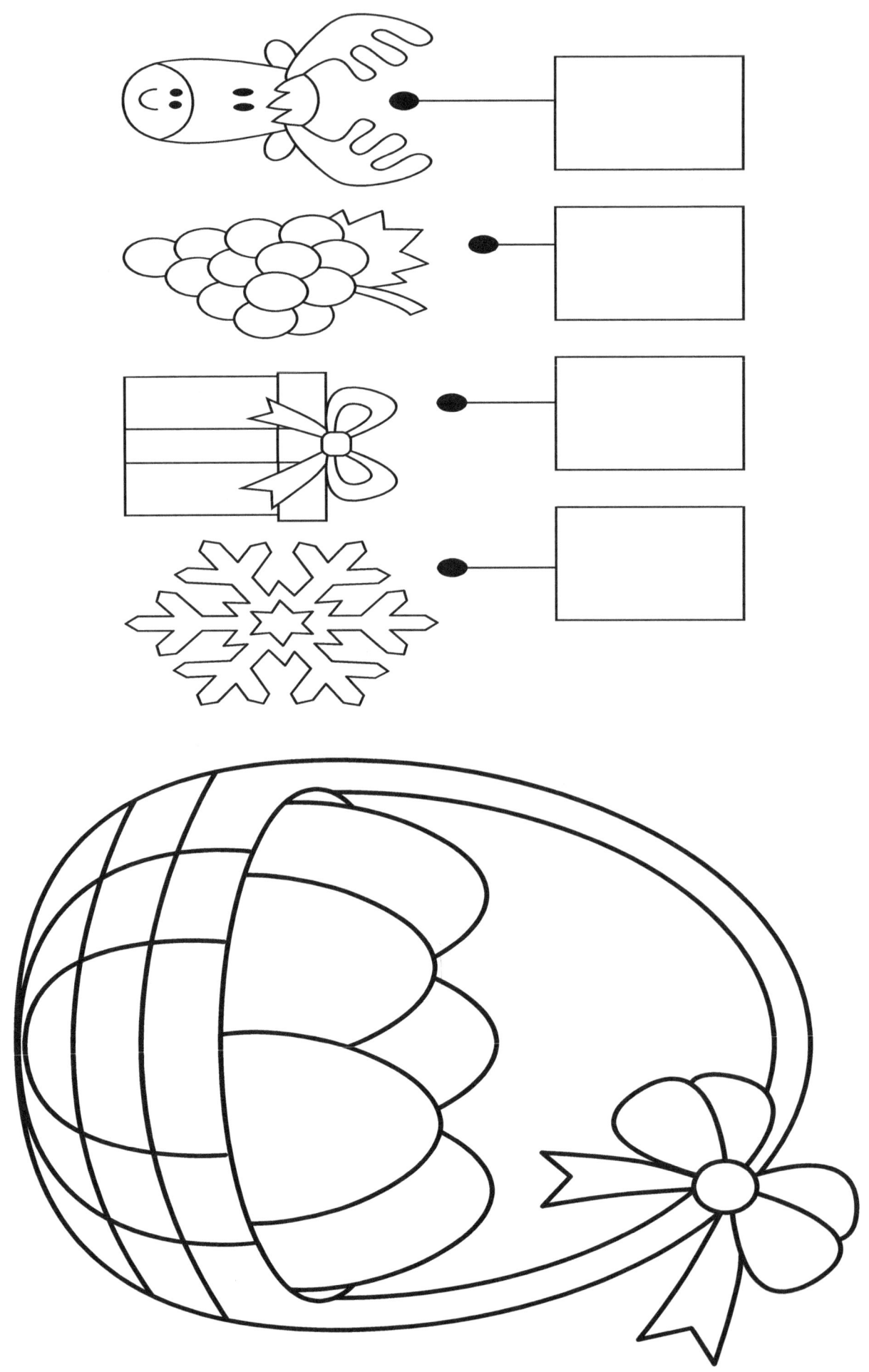

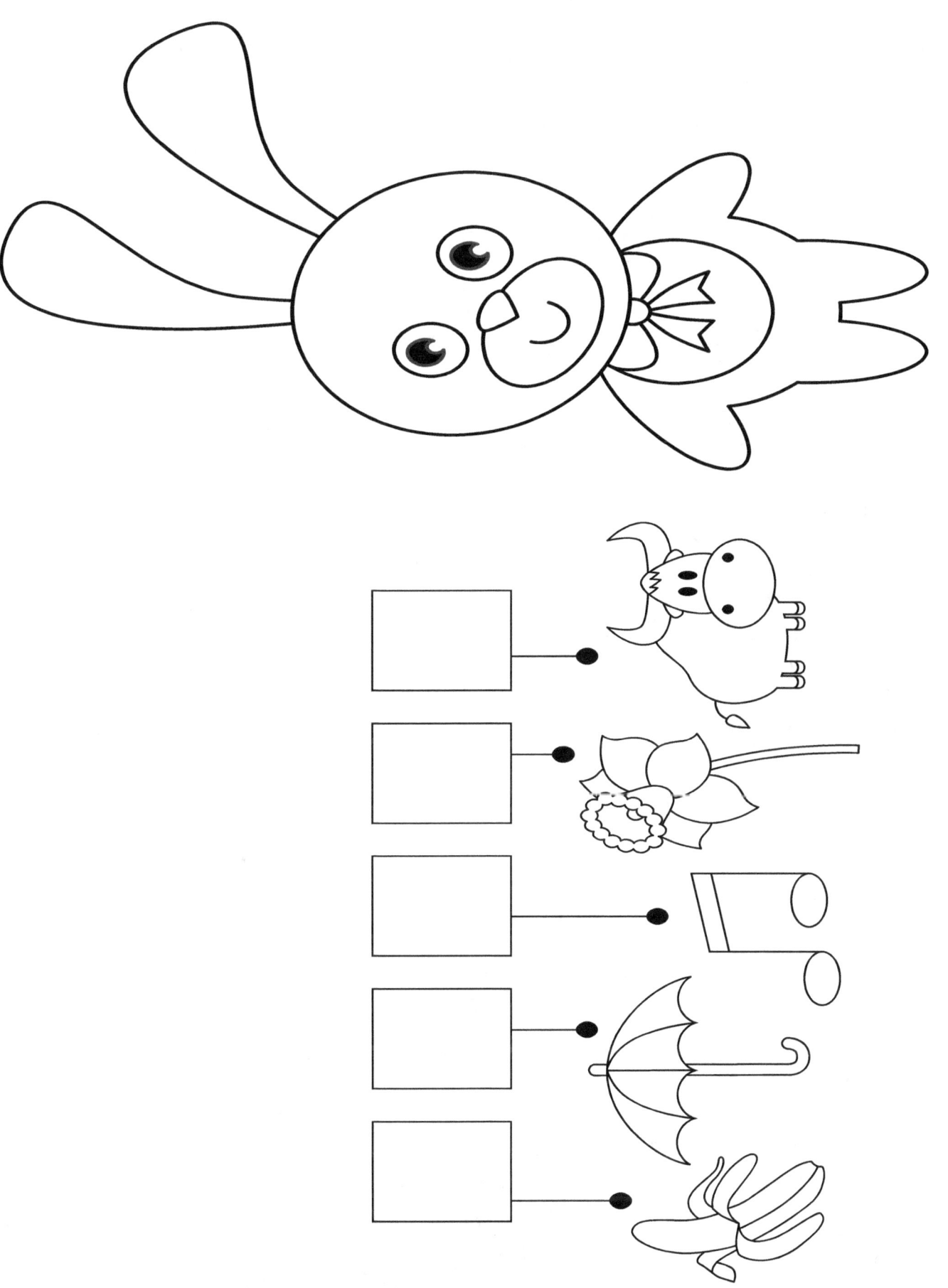

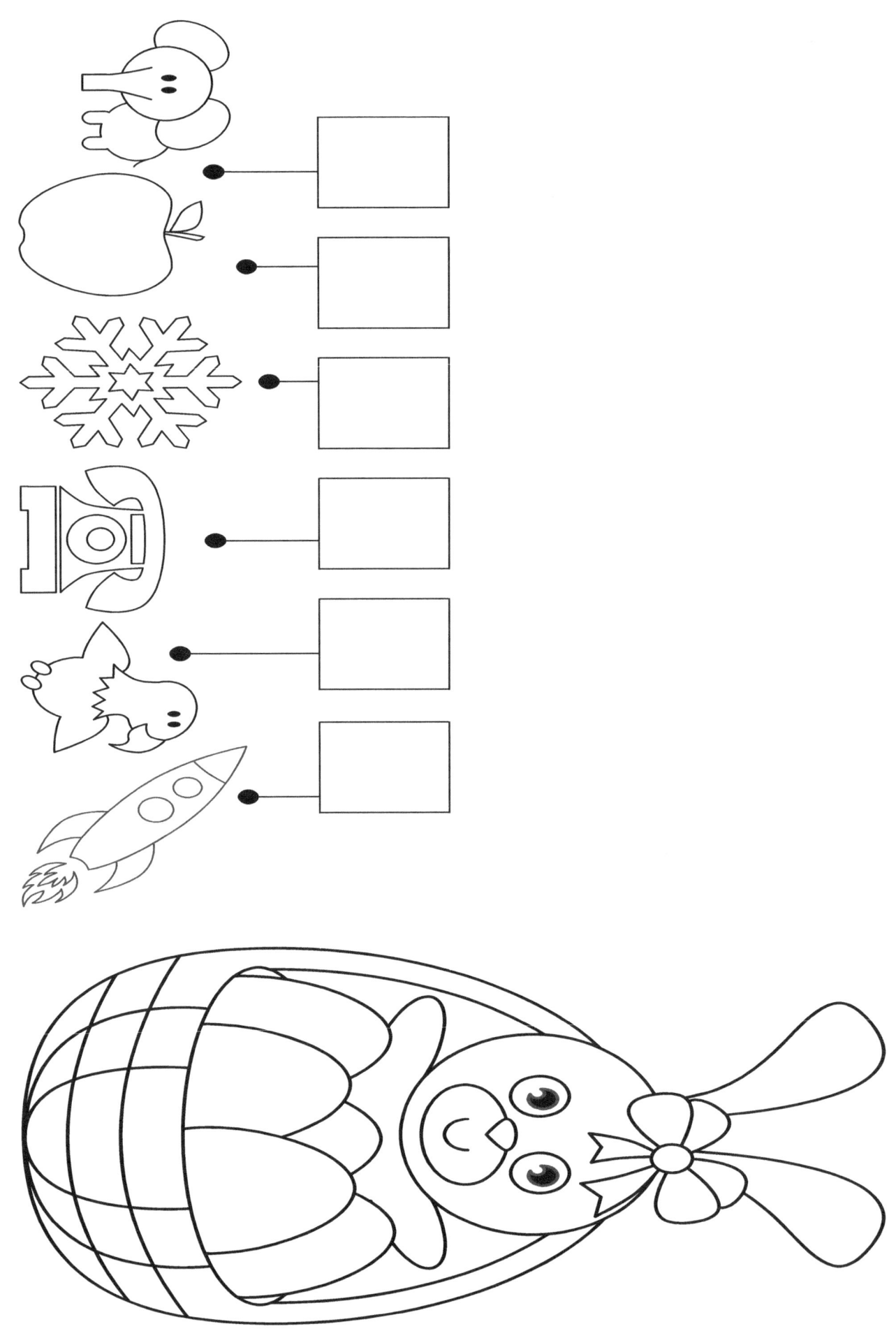

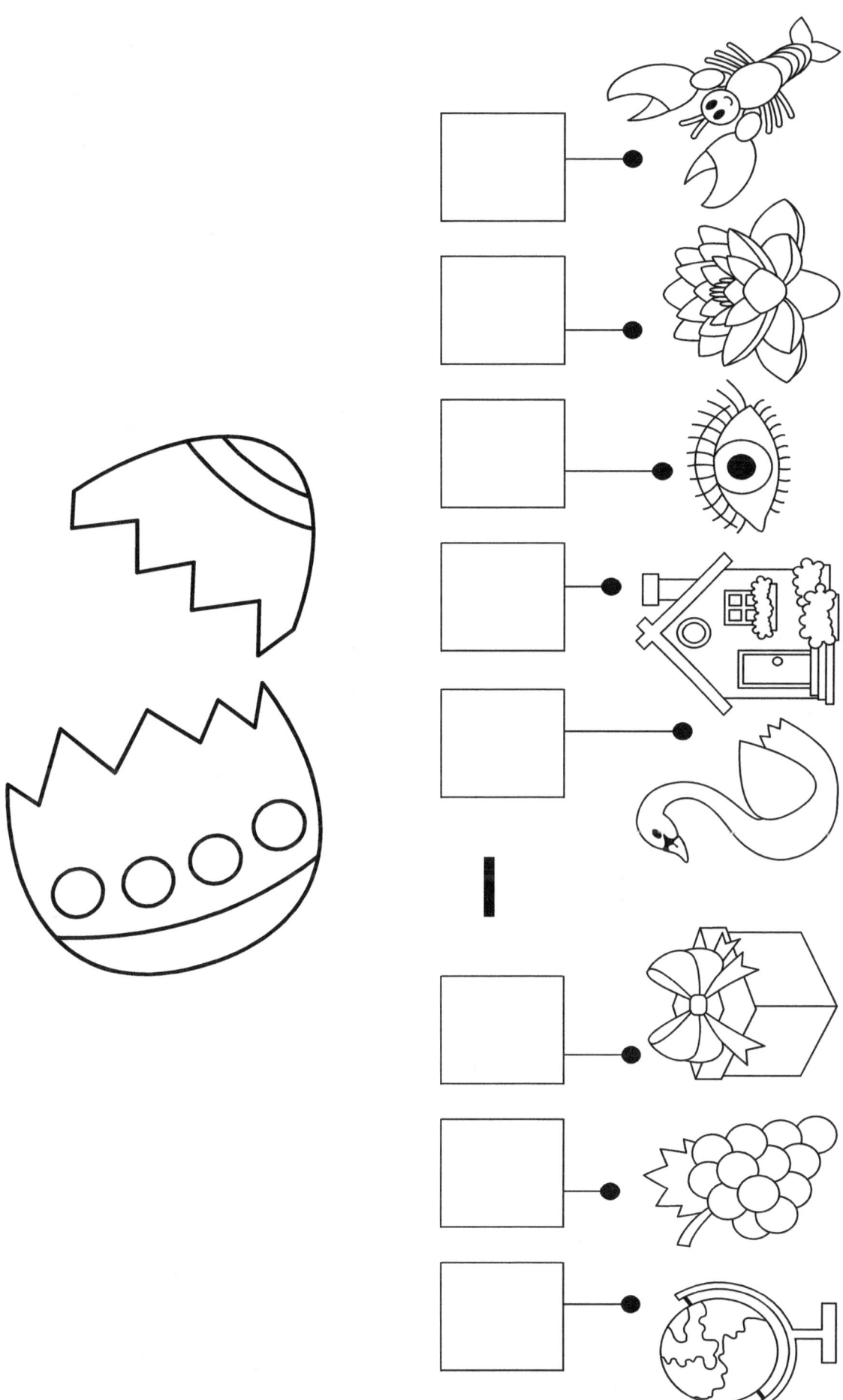

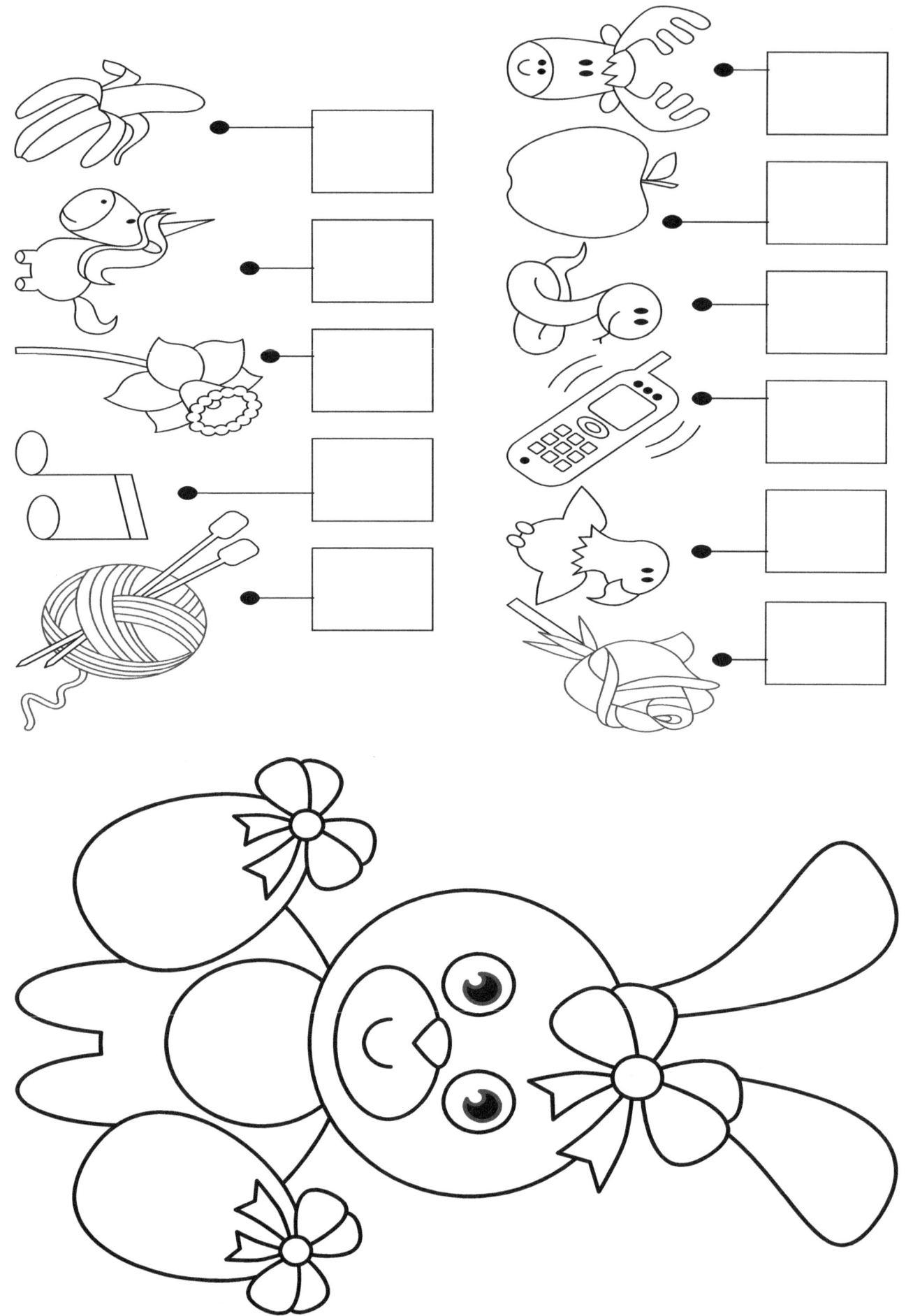

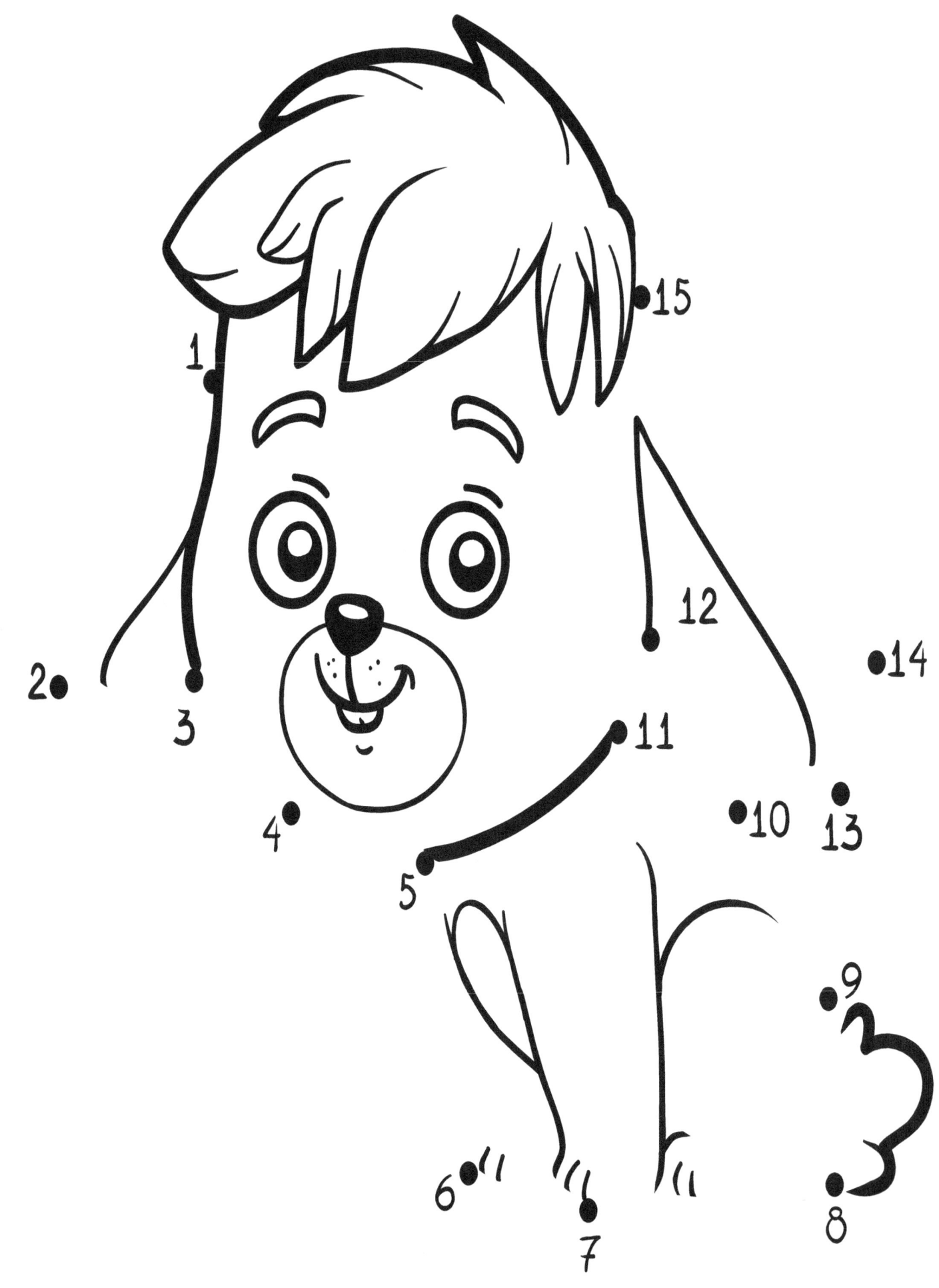

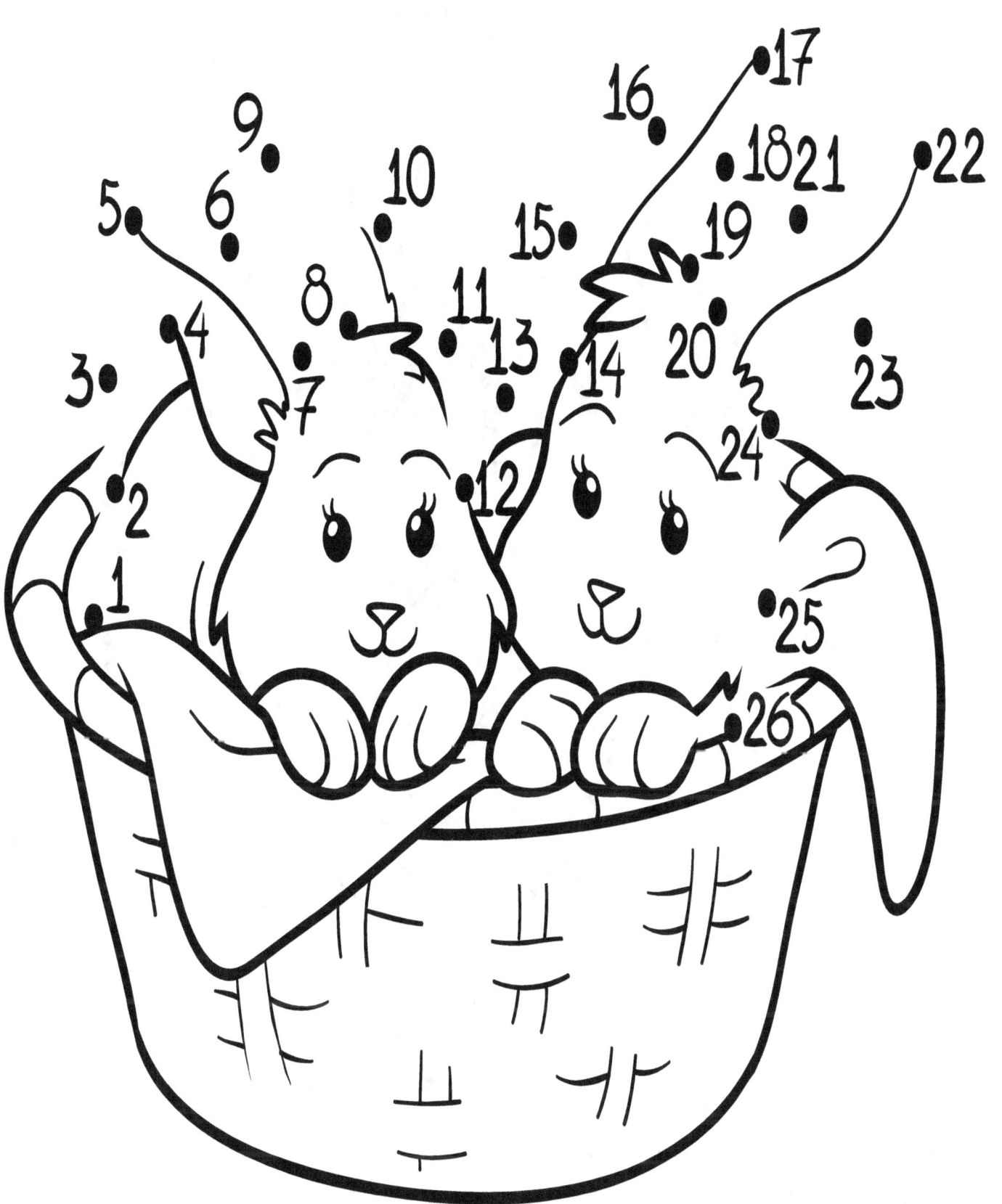

How many rabbits do you see?

How many Easter Bunnies do you see?

How many chickens do you see?

How many Easter Chicks do you see?

ANSWERS

How Many Do You See?

Rabbits ~ 21
Easter Bunnies ~ 18
Chickens ~ 13
Easter Chicks ~ 17

Rebuses

eggs
bunny
Easter
egg-shell
Easter Bunny

adventurelearningpress.com

www.ingramcontent.com/pod-product-compliance
Lightning Source LLC
Chambersburg PA
CBHW081539280526
45788CB00010B/3298